Text copyright 2016 by Rick Camacho

CreateSpace Independent Publishing Platform; 1st edition (January 20, 2016)

All rights reserved.

No part of this publication may be reproduced in whole or in part without written permission of the publisher.

Printed in the U.S.A

*This book is dedicated to my amazing nephew Isaak Brock,
for reminding me that each day is a miracle.*

Contents

1. The Development of Behavior..............8
2. Emotional Chemistry..........................20
3. Shaped by Our Environment................33
4. Time is on our Side...........................42
5. A Diabolical Ideology........................52
6. Emotional Repatterning......................59
7. American Mind Control.....................64
8. Following Authority..........................69
9. The Social Brain..............................76
10. Hypnotherapy and NLP......................89
    - In Conclusion................................99
    - Glossary......................................106
    - Sources.......................................112
    - About the Author...........................114
    - About the SEC LLC........................115

INTRODUCTION

For several years now I have spent countless hours contemplating the complexities of human behavior. What makes people do what they do? How is it, that two people can respond completely different in the exact same situation? During my early teens I began searching for a better way of understanding my mind/body connection and how our mind programs itself with positive and negative thoughts. After years of research I came across a variety of techniques like visualization and positive self-talk, to put myself back in control of my daily behavior. I believe, that the way we act with ourselves and with others truly determines the quality of our lives. Knowing this is empowering because it gives us back control of our minds, instead of handing over control to another person or thing.

Being aware of how other people are behaving and feeling is vitally important in this day and age. Understanding how to adjust your own communication to either direct others toward a desired outcome or to genuinely offer a helping hand in changing their emotional states for the better, is crucial to life. Police Officers, Firefighters, Paramedics, Hostage Negotiators and some Doctors, know that being emotionally flexible and understanding, in certain situations, can save lives and elevate spirits. Every day, researchers are learning more about the chemicals in which the neurons in the human brain use to communicate with each other. We now know that all the feelings and emotions that people experience are produced through chemical reactions in the brain. The "rush" of happiness that a person feels at getting a good grade on a test, winning the lottery, or reuniting with a loved one occur through the brain releasing chemicals such as dopamine and oxytocin into our bodies.

Emotions, such as sadness, grief, and stress have their own chemicals such as cortisol or serotonin. When the brain tells the body to do something, such as to sit down or run, this also sets a chemical process in motion. Repeated exposure to the chemicals that create stress or sadness begin to weaken your body's natural defenses causing you to become more susceptible to viruses, infections and cancers. It is my hope that upon reading this book you will begin to understand that your behaviors don't only effect your social circles, but they also determine the quality of your overall health and vitality.

I am a Hypnotherapist and throughout the years I have used everything from Neuro Linguistic Programming, Guided Imagery and Cognitive Therapy, in order to assist my clients in ridding themselves of deep seeded phobias and limiting beliefs. I've seen the positive effects that these tools for change have had on people's lives. Yet, like any powerful tool in the right hands it can repair, and in the wrong hands it can destroy, it all depends on the intention and moral judgments of the user. One of the reasons for writing this material is to shine a light on those who choose to use these transformative tools for their own personal gain. Cults, are just some of the organizations which have used devious methods to get its members to commit themselves and take part in what may be harmful activities. The sum of these techniques constitutes what many professionals have come to call "Emotional Repatterning." It's also been known as "thought reform," "hypnotic programming", "mental conditioning," and "mind control".

For the past decade, I have dedicated my life to educating and empowering people who have lost their way, so that they may take charge of their own lives and destinies. My hope is that this book will give you a comprehensive and detailed outline of how exactly human behavior is structured, created, manipulated and harnessed, so that you may better understand how to navigate the emotional storms which we as a society face day by day.

1

The Development of Behavior

If there is one thing that I have learned in all my years of studying human behavior, it is that there is more than one way to shape one's perception of the world. Contributors to our worldly perceptions include our family unit, friends, religion, schooling, neighborhood, teachers, life experiences and much more. This is what I have described in my previous books as "you become, who you spend time with". I'm pretty sure that you have heard this before, and you know what? It's true. Have you ever noticed that if you spend a certain amount of time with someone, you begin to adopt certain characteristics from them? Even hours after you leave them, you find yourself talking like them and maybe even moving like them. The worst part about it is that if the person is overly negative it starts to affect your mood, soon you begin using words you wouldn't normally use like, "depressed" or "overwhelmed". I believe I'm someone who took longer than most people to understand this concept. I clung onto relationships with negative people for way too long.

Other people are not the only architects of human behavior. Another factor which greatly shapes us are the significant emotional events that life thrusts upon us. These significant emotional events can be good or bad, expected or unexpected. Good significant emotional events include marriage, having children, job promotions, and coming into wealth. Bad ones are things like divorces, layoffs, financial setbacks, illness and death. These experiences shape what are called our Neuro-Linkages. Neuro-Linkages are the links between thoughts and emotions in our minds, which create and shape our behaviors and performance results .It may sound strange but these neuro-linkages determine how much money you have in the bank, your diet, and your future.

All that you have and are today is created by your actions, which are directly influenced by your neuro-linkages. The mind operates using neuro-linkage principles and does it without any intervention from the conscious mind. We naturally link emotions with thoughts all of the time, every thought is a link to many other thoughts which in turn creates the thinking process. Here's an example: If you think about "money," it is very likely that your next thoughts will be "green," "rich," "house," or "car." Our minds do not link thoughts logically, but purely by our own experiences of life. The freedom to live your own life is dependent on the binds and links between your thoughts. The links between thoughts differ in every person. For one person, the link between "work" and "depression" could be hundreds of times stronger than the link between "work" and "happiness." In the same way, other thoughts are linked including "study" and "benefits," "sports" and "strength," "communication skills" and "success."

In Neuro Linguistic Programming these chain of events are called "anchors". Anchoring refers to the process of associating an internal response with some external or internal trigger so that the response may be quickly, and sometimes covertly, reactivated. Anchoring is a process that on the surface is similar to the "conditioning" technique used by Ivan Pavlov to create a link between the hearing of a bell and salivation in dogs. By associating the sound of a bell with the act of giving food to his dogs, Pavlov found he could eventually just ring the bell and the dogs would start salivating, even though no food was given. A remembered picture may become an anchor for a particular internal feeling, a touch on the leg may become an anchor for a visual fantasy or even a belief. In Neuro Linguistic Programming an anchor becomes a tool for reactivating the mental processes associated with creativity, learning, concentration and other important resources.

The process of establishing an anchor or a neuro-linkage basically involves associating two experiences together in time. In behavioral conditioning models, associations become more strongly established through repetition. Repetition may also be used to strengthen anchors as well. For example, most cases of post-traumatic stress disorder involve the stimulating of an emotional trigger. If let's say a war veteran, comes back home and is thrown into a nervous state every time a car backfires or has a panic attack whenever they are in a group of people this is clearly an indication that a neuro linkage has begun to change their behavior in some way. In fact, this happens more often than people think.

Unfortunately, although these neuro-linkages are meant to protect us, they sometimes install false beliefs which eventually create destructive results. If one day you eat a hot dog and suddenly become the victim of accidental food poisoning, the next time you get near a hot dog, even though you rationally know this is a different hot dog in a completely different situation, you will still have either an emotional or physical reaction to it. Often times just thinking about something that has made you sick in the past can retrigger the same emotions in you. This is how people can develop fears of public speaking, swimming, heights, driving cars and even speaking to a certain type of person. If a particular man or woman in anyway reminds you of someone who has hurt or lied to you in the past you might have an instant distrust or dislike of the person without really even knowing them. This is where a lot of racism and general prejudice stems from.

The Impact of Mirror-Neurons on Behavior

Neuro-Linkages are not purely psychological like some people have come to believe, they are also neurological. Scientists have now acknowledged the existence of what are being called Mirror- Neurons. Mirror-Neurons are brain cells that cause someone to perform a certain action when they witness someone else perform the same action. This in mainly how very young children learn how to laugh, smile, walk, talk etc. In the late 1980's a group of researchers wanted to learn more about how these neurons responded to different objects and actions, so they used sensors attached to a male monkey's brain to record activity from individual mirror neurons while giving the monkey different objects to handle.

Soon something very surprising occurred, when the researchers picked up an object to hand to the monkey, some of the monkey's motor neurons would start to fire. Even more surprisingly, these were the same neurons that would also fire when the monkey grasped the object himself. It was found that individual neurons would only respond to very specific actions.

The mirror neuron that would fire when, say, the monkey grasped a banana would also fire as he watched the experimenter grasp a banana. In another study scientists monitored the brainwave activity of 9 male participants as they inhaled noxious odors as they viewed a film of an actor wrinkling up his face into a disgusted look. The researchers found that both feeling disgusted and watching someone else look disgusted activated a particular segment of the participants' brain.

Our minds are fast learning machines. Which is why by the age of 6, most children have already begun creating their own personalities by piecing together strips of behavior which they observe from a variety of sources. Seeing how dad reacts when he's angry and how mom deals with stress begins creating a baseline of consciousness that predicts how the child will react in the same situation in the future.

Some parents I've encountered take it for granted that children model their behaviors, so when a parent comes to me and says "I don't know why my son always misbehaves when he doesn't get what he wants" my response is to get the parents to become more aware of the kind of behaviors the child is exposed to around the house. Now I understand that after 6 years of age it's extremely hard to monitor everything your child does, especially with TV, Internet and the influence of other children, but this just points out how important the first couple of years are in the mental development process.

Marshmallows In Scientific Research

One very famous experiment in particular chronicled exactly how crucial behavioral development is in early adolescents. The famed "Marshmallow Experiment" was conducted in the 1970's and centered on testing over two hundred children between the ages of 3 and 6 for early signs of self-control. In the experiment each child was encouraged to participate in a game or test, if the child got the answer right they were rewarded with a marshmallow. They were then given a choice, either eat the treat now, or, if they could hold out for another 10 minutes until the researcher returned, they could have two. Most children said they would wait. But some failed to resist the pull of temptation for even a minute. Many others struggled a little longer before eventually giving in. The most successful participants figured out how to distract themselves from the treat's seduction by turning around, covering their eyes or kicking the desk therefore delaying gratification for the full 10 minutes.

After the experiment, over the course of two decades the researchers kept track of each child in the study and found that those who were able to wait the 10 minutes were significantly less likely to have problems with behavior, drug addiction or obesity by the time they were in high school, compared with kids who gobbled the snack in less than a minute. Experiments such as this one, in my opinion act as an "early warning detection system" for parents. I encourage all new parents to try this out with their own toddlers. If you conduct your own "marshmallow experiment" I'm certain it will give you a strong insight into the behaviors your child has been exposed to so far, giving you the ability to improve upon your child's behavior before it becomes that much harder later on.

Psychology has the tendency to study people by using a medical model, as if something is broken and you have to fix it, not as if it's something that is learned. If you look at behavior as learned, you can say that you are a product of your history, but in fact you don't have to be. The fact that someone grew up being afraid of something doesn't mean that they will always be afraid. If you change the way in which you think about it, you can begin to reprogram your subconscious mind. As human beings, we have imagination under our control, if you use your imagination in a structured way then you begin to restructure the way you think and the way you feel. In life, we don't always have a choice of how people talk to us, but we do have a choice about how we respond to it. Visualization is important, but what's even more important is the feeling it creates inside of you. Create powerful images, and you'll create powerful emotional states. Below I have included a very powerful visualization technique that can change your life.

The Behavior Changer Exercise

1.) Think of a feeling or behavior that you would like to change. This format is particularly useful in dealing with feelings that seem to compel people to act in ways that do not match their self-image.

2.) Close your eyes and see what happens from an associated point of view. If it is behavior, identify the trigger point of the sequence. Put a border around it and make it bright and intense.

3.) Now see yourself (dissociated) as if you have already made the change. See how you will be acting, hear what you will be hearing. Ensure this scenario is preferable to your previous one.

4.) Shrink the image of your desired state down to a small, dark square, and place it in the corner of the first image you made.

5.) Now, darken and shrink the large image down as you simultaneously brighten and enlarge the second image until it completely covers the first one. Open your eyes to "break trance". Repeat this exercise several times.

2

Emotional Chemistry

In the past several decades, researchers have begun to understand the chemistry and biology of love, hate, stress, depression, fear, ecstasy and many other strong emotions. At the center of how our bodies respond to love and affection is a hormone called oxytocin. Most of our oxytocin is made in the area of the brain called the hypothalamus. Some is released into our bloodstream, but much of its effect is thought to reside in the brain.

Oxytocin makes us feel good when we're close to family and other loved ones. It does this by acting through what scientists call the dopamine reward system. Dopamine is a brain chemical that plays a crucial part in how we perceive pleasure. Many drugs of abuse act through this system.

Problems with the system can lead to serious depression and other mental illness. Oxytocin does more than make us feel good. It lowers the levels of stress hormones in the body, reducing blood pressure, improving mood, increasing tolerance for pain and it even speeds up your bodies healing process.

It also seems to play an important role in our relationships, oxytocin has been linked, for example, to how much we trust others. One thing researchers all agree on is that physical contact changes oxytocin levels. People who get lots of hugs and other warm contact at home tend to have the highest levels of oxytocin. Frequent warm contact may somehow prime the oxytocin system and make it quicker to turn on whenever there's warm contact.

The same holds true for mothers and infants. They both produce higher levels of oxytocin when they have lots of contact with each other. Much of what we know about oxytocin today has come from research in animals. Mother rats, for instance, can stimulate oxytocin in their pups by licking and grooming them. This loving care has long-term effects. When researchers separate pups from their mothers for 10-15 minutes a day and then reunite them, many mothers are so glad to see their pups that they lick and groom them intensively. If the separation lasts for several hours, however, it can have the opposite effect, the mother won't lick and groom her pups.

Some mothers just never lick and groom their pups when they come back. Pups that are groomed a lot when they're reunited with their mothers become more comfortable exploring new environments. The ignored ones develop more anxiety disorders, produce higher levels of stress hormones and have higher blood pressure. Research from other animals, including monkeys, confirms that the quality of care a mother gives her offspring can have long-term effects on their personality characteristics and mental health as well as physical problems like heart disease.

Understanding Your Mental Process

Every time you have a thought you make a chemical. This immaterial thing called a thought fires circuits in your brain, and the brain releases chemicals so we can feel exactly how we're thinking. So, if you have negative thoughts or unhappy thoughts in a matter of seconds you begin feeling negative or unworthy. Your thoughts then signal your body to feel the way you think, and because the brain is in constant communication with the body it's always evaluating the internal environment. Once the brain notices it's feeling a certain way we tend to think the way we feel, which then makes more chemicals to feel the way we think and think the way we feel, until we create what is called a state of being. If a person can't think greater than how they feel, they'll never change. So to change then, is actually to think greater than how you feel, which in turn begins to produce new chemicals in your body. In other words, if a person has been depressed for years, then their body is chemically trained to respond to and to produce depression chemicals like cortisone and serotonin.

This explains why change can be so hard. You are not only fighting years of mental programming, but you are also going against the emotional cocktail that your body has grown accustomed to. High emotions like love and sadness, then become as addictive as cigarettes, alcohol and drugs, because when it comes down to it, love, hate, passion, depression and euphoria are in fact all drugs that our brains create within the body in a matter of seconds. Repeated exposure to the sadness chemical cortisol can also have a very damaging effect on the body. Not only does cortisol over time begin to weaken your immune system, but it also starts a process that can eventually lead to organ failure.

In order to retrain our body chemically we must do what many of the self-help gurus call "acting as if". This method of therapy has not only changed my life for the better, but it has also aided my client's in ridding themselves of long standing mental blocks, fears, phobias and general feelings of inadequacy. This method works because it forces a person to literally break the habit of being themselves. Once you begin acting a certain way for a long period of time your brain literally reprograms your subconscious mind to take on this new personality. If you have a severe problem with self-esteem and you begin to stand, talk and do things you think a confident person would do, then you begin to override your old programming. At first it's going to feel awkward, you might even question your ability to accomplish this, but stick to it I know first-hand that it works.

Growing up I had big problem with self-esteem, I was so bad I could barely step out of the house. I started working on myself, reading motivational books going to seminars forcing myself to talk to people. Then I stumbled upon the "act as if" philosophy. The first couple of times I practiced this method, nothing seemed to work, but the more I tried, the more I noticed drastic changes in my own behavior.

Some of you may find this much more difficult to do because it's such a new sensation, but I encourage you stick with it. If you are a shy person start by practicing 10 minutes a day just standing and moving like a confident person, back straight, shoulders up. After a couple of days, I promise, everything will start to fall into place. Practice is the key when it comes to reprogramming your behaviors, you can't take a break, which is why I have included a step by step exercise for you to use.

The Modeling Technique

- ➤ Choose a "Role Model", someone whose performance you would like to replicate. Spend as much time as possible studying your chosen role model in the flesh or on DVD, videos and voice recordings. Simply relax while you do this and absorb as much information as possible.
- ➤ When you feel as familiar as possible with your role model's performance, close your eyes, relax and recreate your role model performing a

sequence of actions at the highest level of excellence that you desire.

- When you have watched this performance for some time, move around the mental image of your role model and step inside their body. Imagine you are able to see through their eyes, hear through their ears and feel how they feel.
- Run through the same sequence of actions but from within, noticing this time how your body feels as you do this. Repeat this several times until you have a feeling of familiarity.
- Step out of your role model's body with the intention of retaining as much of the energy, confidence and body sensations you felt while you were inside.
- As soon as possible and as much as possible practice the barrowed skill, noticing how the exercise improves your performance.
- Repeat the entire exercise, combing it with whatever real-time practice you do, at least once a day for the first month, then at least once a week as maintenance.

How you feel at any moment in time is the result of how you are using your own mind and body. No matter what happens in your life, you are in control of your own state of mind. People in our society often turn to external means such as food, alcohol, cigarettes or drugs to change their mood, this often works because it momentarily alters your brains chemistry, but the long term effects of such methods can cause major problems in your health, relationships and work life. This is why I strongly recommend "acting as if" as the best and healthiest alternative to instantly and effectively changing your behaviors and actions for the better.

The human mind has a very interesting way of sorting information so that the events in our lives are always matched to our resident beliefs for the sole purpose of assisting in making sense out of life. On any given day, the brain is scanning every experience we have, searching for anything that could possibly match up with our existing beliefs. Information is sifted, weighed and valued in a precise search for the information that gives confirmation to our present belief systems. When a match is identified, the brain collects it and accepts it as truth. Other information which doesn't fit is distorted or deleted.

Limiting or mistaken beliefs are nurtured and verified in the same way as good or helpful beliefs. If you have a belief that states "I don't deserve to be happy" then life will always seem to put happiness out of your reach. Positive beliefs offer opposite results. Life is doing nothing more than giving us what we believe, our beliefs are creating our good or bad luck by getting us to notice the information that matches our beliefs.

When someone believes "I am not good enough", every criticism given to them is immediately taken as a complete truth rather than just another's opinion. Because the person is in a heightened state of awareness even a raised eye brow can be interpreted as "I knew it, they think I'm not good enough" rather than," I wonder if they have a question?" Every mistake is seen as evidence of "not being good enough" rather than seeing it simply as an opportunity to learn.

The good news is that the human mind does the same diligent job with positive beliefs. So if you had the positive belief "I am successful", the brain would search out anything that could possibly fit in with that belief. Phrases such as, "You can do anything you set your mind to" would be eligible to match up. Of course, any direct positive comment will also be recognized by the brain as a match, such as, "You've done very well"; "That was a great try" or "You really have a natural ability for that".

Beliefs really do have a profound influence on our lives, not just socially but physically too. During the Second World War, due to the massive amount of wounded soldiers, military clinics ran out of morphine. Desperate to keep the peace among the wounded men, the medics decided to continue telling the men that they were being given morphine, although they were in reality injecting the men with a water based saline solution. Immediately afterwards, more than 70% percent of the wounded soldiers reported that the saline treatment, which they believed to be morphine, eased their pain tremendously. Today, scientists now understand why those soldiers felt better. The army medics gave the soldiers a placebo, which is a substance that may look like real medication, but in fact is not. Placebos can take many forms, the most common are sugar pills, devices, procedures or even just a doctor telling a patient that he or she will soon feel better. Exactly how placebos work to relieve pain and other symptoms can be explained by neuroscience. When activated by the power of belief, placebos can cause the brain to release its own pain relief chemicals, in fact, research shows blocking these chemicals can prevent placebo effects. In addition, brain areas that process pain show reduced activity following placebo treatment. One study showed that men were more likely to report relief from heat induced arm pain when they thought a fake anesthetic numbing cream was the real thing. Imaging data revealed that the placebo effect had suppressed incoming pain signals from the arm to the brain.

Upon further examination, the placebo effect appears to depend primarily on a combination of verbal suggestions, observational cues, and mental conditioning. These factors create expectations that then influence the placebo effect by activating the brain's dopamine reward centers. When people believe that a placebo is a real drug, either because they've been told it's the real thing or it looks real enough, the brain produces more dopamine.

The biological effects of a placebo, therefore, are similar to those of other pleasurable activities, such as eating when hungry or drinking when thirsty. Conditioning, the process by which we become trained that one thing happens as a result of another, also plays a role in the placebo effect. If patients believe that a particular therapy will ease their symptoms, then they are more likely to experience relief when they believe they are receiving that therapy again, even if they are actually experiencing the placebo effect.

3

Shaped By Our Environment

Now that we understand that we form our future behaviors by modeling the people around us, mainly our parents, we must also be aware that the environment also plays a massive role in how you will behave at any moment in time. This fact may at times cause a person to act contradictory to their own beliefs.

Let's just say, that one of your strongest beliefs is that you would never ever harm or murder anyone, then one day in order to defend a loved one from a crazed maniac you jump into the situation and do whatever is necessary to keep your family safe, which includes killing the maniac in self-defense. Or better yet, you join the military to defend your country, during the heat of battle you kill several of your country's enemies. Upon the end of your tour, you come back a hero and are embraced by your family and nation. Now, let's say a private citizen with no affiliations to any military, hops on a plane goes over to the war zone and takes several enemy lives in the process. Does he come back a hero? Not a chance, the citizen returns labeled as a murderer and is locked away in a cold cell for the rest of his life. I am in no way advocating the use of violence, I'm using the above example to get the point across to you that our behaviors are also governed by the outside laws and or customs of your environment. What is seen as evil in one nation may be perceived as a necessary good in another. It all comes down to a matter of what is called environmental perception.

One of my absolute favorite examples of the above principles on situational perception is what was called "The Stanford Prison Experiment" which was conducted in 1971 at Stanford University. The experiment was a psychological study of the human response to captivity. The subjects were randomly assigned to take on the role of either "prisoner" or "guard". The participants who were assigned to play the role of a guard were given sticks and sunglasses, while those assigned to act as prisoners were arrested by the city police, deloused, made to wear chains and prison cloths, and were eventually transported to the bottom level of the Stanford psychology department, which had been converted into a mock jail by the researchers.

The study, which was planned as a two week experiment became progressively more sadistic, as the subjects playing the guards became more and aggressive toward the prisoners. After only a couple of days the bold study very quickly got out of hand. A mini-riot broke out on the second day. One prisoner in particular developed a psychosomatic rash all over his body upon finding out that his so-called "parole" had been turned down. After only 6 days, the experiment came to a screeching halt, do to fear that one of the prisoners would be seriously injured.

Several decades later, the results of this remarkable experiment have aided psychologists in forming what is now being called "Situational Psychology" which is being used to explain such tragedies as Guantanamo Bay and the much more recent Abu Ghraib incidents. The horrendous human rights violations that occurred at the Abu Ghraib prison under the authority of the United States shows strong comparisons to "The Stanford Prison Experiment". The American soldiers at Abu Ghraib, which were all reservists at the time, were thrust into the roles of prison guards and subsequently began to show signs of aggression which led many of them to cruelly torture prisoners. Several of the specific methods of humiliation conducted at Abu Ghraib were similar to those that occurred in the Stanford Prison Experiment.

An Analysis of Social Conditioning

Most people believe that the choices they make result from a rational analysis of available alternatives. In reality, however, emotions greatly influence and, in many cases, even determine our decisions. When we are confronted with a decision, emotions from previous related experiences direct what we are considering. These emotions create preferences which lead to our decision. Emotions are the primary reason why consumers prefer brand name products. After all, many of the products we buy are available as generic brands with the same ingredients and at cheaper prices. Why do we decide to pay more for brand name products? The main reason is that a nationally advertised brand has power in the marketplace because it creates an emotional connection to the consumer.

A brand is nothing more than a mental representation of a product in the consumer's mind. If the representation consists only of the product's attributes, features, and other information, there are no emotional links to influence consumer preference and action. The richer the emotional content of a brand's mental representation, the more likely the consumer will be a loyal user.

While emotion can be communicated effectively in a print ad or television commercial, there are other important components of a brand which have emotional dimensions. For example, rich and powerful mental representations of a brand include its personality. Consumers perceive the same type of personality characteristics in brands as they do in other people, and just like with people, they are attracted more to, some personality types than others. Brand personality is communicated by marketers through packaging, visual imagery, and the types of words used to describe the brand. Another important foundation for a brand's emotions can be found in its "narrative", the story that communicates "who" it is, what it means to the consumer, and why the consumer should care.

This narrative is the main basis for brand advertising and promotion. For consumers, perhaps the most important characteristic of emotions is that they push us toward action. In response to an emotion, humans are compelled to do something. In a physical confrontation, fear forces us to choose between "fight or flight" to insure our self-preservation. In our daily social confrontations, insecurity may cause us to buy the latest iPhone to support our positive self-identity. We as a whole must become more aware of the constant influence that these advertisement companies are having on us, and it's my hope that this book will begin to open your eyes to the affects that these methods are having on us.

Advertising companies are not the only one's using the principles of "social conditioning". Every time you are inspired by a charismatic speaker or are persuaded to vote on a specific topic you are being directed without your knowledge. Political speeches most often contain persuasive language patterns often used in hypnotherapy and neuro linguistic programming. Some of the most popular methods used in these speeches have names like, hypnotic anchoring, pacing and leading, distraction and utilization, stacked language patterns and pre-programmed response adaptation.

Once upon a time these techniques were only used by hypnotherapists to help their client's get passed certain limitations and trigger motivation, but now nearly every CEO or political leader uses these powerful tools for personal gain. Political techniques are at the height of deception and psychological manipulation, yet these methods still remain hidden because one must understand and be aware of the language patterns in order to spot them.

Most political figures are not just using subliminal messages, but textbook covert hypnosis techniques on audiences that are intentionally designed to side-line rational judgment and implant subconscious commands so you will think they are wonderful and vote them into office. These subconscious techniques have been proven to elicit powerful emotions from audiences' side-lining rational judgment. Here are some ways to tell if someone is attempting to use hypnotic language on you.

- ✓ Be cautious of permissive language. "Feel free to be happy." "You're welcome to test drive this motorcycle if you like." "You can enjoy this as much as you want." Watch out for this.

- ✓ Be cautious of gibberish. Nonsense phrases like "As you release this feeling more and more you will find yourself moving into present alignment with the sound of your success more and more." This kind of gibberish is the bread and butter of the pacing-and-leading phase of covert persuasion tactics, the person isn't actually saying anything, they're just trying to program your internal emotional states and move you towards where they want you to go.
- ✓ Read between the lines. Hypnotic language patterns will consistently use language with hidden or layered meanings. For instance "Diet, nutrition and sleep with me are the most important things, don't you think?" On the surface, if you heard this sentence quickly, it would seem like an obvious statement that you would probably agree with without much thought. Yes, of course diet, nutrition and sleep are important things, sure, and this person's really into being healthy, that's great. But what's the layered-in message? "Diet, nutrition

and sleep with me are the most important things, don't you think?" Yep, and you just unconsciously agreed to it. Skilled persuaders can be incredibly subtle with this.

4
Time Is On Our Side

One of the newest and most exciting fields in psychology today is what is being called "Time Perspective Types" or "Time Psychology", which is the study of how individuals divide the flow of their personal experience into specific time zones. Planning and achieving future goals can't happen unless a person is future focused, experiencing consistent feelings of guilt and revenge are based on constantly looking to the past, while impulsivity and improvisation is a focus on present orientation.

Men and women who make decisions based entirely on the situation they are currently in, are generally considered present oriented, those who draw upon past experiences to help them make decisions, are past oriented, people who weigh consequences and plan out their year ahead of time are future oriented. No one is entirely one thing, in any given moment you can jump back and forth from past, present and future perspectives, but most people have one type of time orientation which dominates most of the decisions that govern their lives. There are actually six main "time zones" that people live in which I've included below.

1) Past- Positive Focused
2) Past- Negative Focused
3) Present- Hedonistic
4) Present-Fatalist
5) Future-Goal Oriented
6) Future-Transcendental-Life After Death

People who are past focused either remember all the good old times or all the bad times, they are called past-positives or past negatives. Then there are the present oriented people. Those who are present hedonistic live for pleasure and are more likely to develop bad habits such as drug abuse, alcoholism and depression. Then there are those who are present oriented because they believe that there is no use in planning because their lives are fated toward a specific direction. Future oriented people who resist instant gratification and focus on goal setting and lifelong projects are future goal oriented, then there are future-transcendental focused individuals who primarily concern themselves with life after death and leaving their mortal body.

Visionaries Are Future-Goal Oriented

Some of the greatest inventors, innovators and leaders in history have been individuals who were able to mentally construct a consistent view of the future they desired most. After nearly 10,000 failed attempts to make the light bulb Thomas A. Edison finally succeeded in making his vision a reality by constantly picturing what his invention would look, feel and even sound like. By daily mental rehearsal men like Edison, Nicola Tesla and The Wright Brothers were able to manifest their dreams and break down borders, leaving it open for others to follow in their creative wake. John F. Kennedy is famously quoted as saying "Change is the law of life, and those who only look to the past or present are certain to miss the future". Just by this quote alone you can already tell that President Kennedy was a strong future-goal oriented person, which is why in my opinion, he was able to initiate so much change in such a short time.

Understanding what your primary time perspective is puts you in the driver's seat, awareness is the key. If you are struggling with things in your life at the moment, I encourage you to take a look at what time perspective you are currently using and make a shift. A very close friend of mine named Jack, (not his real name) had been struggling for years with a crippling addiction to spending. Jack had a very good paying job but every time he would get paid he would instantly go out and spend his money, living paycheck to paycheck had become a normal thing for him, that is until an unexpected financial emergency caused him to open his eyes.

After a few hours of working with him we both came to the realization that his time perspective was present hedonist with a dash of past negative, which together is a recipe for life long failure and pain. I spent the next few weeks working with Jack. First I sat him down and made him visualize what his life would be like in five years if he didn't change his behavior. He saw himself broke, homeless lonely and depressed. Then I made him visual the opposite, a bright positive future. Next we created a five year plan for his life, which included budgeting his income, saving up for a house then eventually proposing to his girlfriend. I'm happy to report that now two years after changing his time perspective, Jack has not only been promoted twice at work but he and his new wife have just put down a down payment for their dream home.

Setting goals is a fundamental component to long-term success. The basic reason for this is that you can't get where you are trying to go until you clearly define where that is. Research studies show a direct link between goals and enhanced performance in business, just like in Jack's case, once he shifted his attention from present to future he began to excel at work and his confidence doubled. Goals help you focus and allocate your time and resources efficiently, and they can keep you motivated when you feel like giving up. Goals help employees stay aware of what is expected from them and leave little room for people to hide behind the curtain of unspecified expectations. Furthermore, setting and achieving goals translates to feelings of success for both individuals and companies, which in turn spurs greater productivity and confidence. Below I have included five guidelines everyone should keep in mind as they write out their goals.

1. Make sure you really want it. A goal should be emotionally satisfying. It should tug at your heart strings. Make sure that you really want to accomplish the goals that you set. In order to become committed to a goal, one must believe in its importance or significance.

2. Make sure the goal is feasible. You should be able to visualize and taste the result you are after. By visualizing your success with close attention to detail, you are preparing yourself and making sure you take the steps necessary to get there. You can also recite positive affirmations to get you in the right emotional state.

3. Make sure the goal is in your hands. This means you must be able to achieve the goal as a result of your own hard work and determination, or with the willing assistance of someone already in your social network. If you have no control over the outcome, it does not make for a realistic goal. Unrealistic goals can ultimately lead to depression and low feelings of self-worth. There must be an action, or several actions, you can perform which will enable you to achieve the goals you set.

4. Be flexible. Watch your progress periodically, provide honest feedback and adjust as you go along. If you encounter roadblocks on your path to achieving your goals, don't give up. Instead, be willing to alter them to meet your new needs. Don't become rigid in accomplishing something that is no longer relevant to you or your business just for the sake of your ego. Sometimes knowing when to walk away or shift gears is progress in and of itself.

5. Write down your goals. A written goal represents a real commitment. Commitment is what separates our dreams from our goals. Keep a copy of your goal plan in sight and refer to it often. The secret behind making a real effort, is in the development of habits and strategies which support the achievement of clear goals. Successful people form habits to do the things that less successful people don't like to do

Whether you want to lose weight, start a relationship with someone or set out on a spiritual awakening, setting a specific time frame increases your chances of actually accomplishing what you've set out to accomplish. Be as thorough as possible when you write out your goals, list the time, day, place and even the desired state of mind you want to attain upon the completion of your goal.

The most important aspect of all is to really have a crystal clear image in your mind of what you want or how you want to be. Challenge yourself to develop a grand vision for your future. Another very effective way of motivating yourself is to use the power of negative imagery as I did with my friend Jack. Most people use negative pictures to dissuade themselves from doing what they really want to do, but by using this technique in another way it can bring very positive results to your life. Let's say someone you know is trying to stop smoking and is not responding to other smoking therapies, what you have them do is to vividly picture themselves in the near future consumed with all the negative effects smoking cigarettes can offer. Have them sit down close their eyes and picture their skin old and leathery, their teeth yellow and stained from the smoke, have them visualize a breathing tube sticking out from their throat. The key here is to make the experience feel as real as possible. Instruct them to see and feel how their weak body, which is now filled with cancer, struggles to walk across the room. The more into detail you go the better.

The point of this technique is to deliver a massive shock of realism to a person's nervous system, with the intention of interrupting their dominant negative habit patterns. This technique can also be used to help someone reevaluate whether a current course of action should be changed or adjusted. One of my clients, I'll call her Betty, was wondering if she should stay in her current job which was paying her very well or accept a position in another company that paid her less but was more in tuned with her life goals and personality.

I sat her down and had her visualize what she would be like in five years if she decided to stay in her current position. After a few minutes I had Betty open her eyes for a few minutes then I ran her through the exercise again but this time in the perceptive of her working in this new field. After an hour or so of this back and forth mental rehearsal she decided to try her hand at this new career which till this day has drastically improved her living situation. I encourage all of you to follow in Jack and Betty's footsteps for the sole purpose of taking control of your future instead of handing control over to outside influences.

5

A Diabolical Ideology

If I were to ask you all who you thought was the cruelest, most sadistic and murderous man of the twentieth century, I am certain that at least 70 % of you would say Adolf Hitler. Hitler's grotesque and ruthless deeds have become common knowledge. In fact the name's Adolf and Hitler have both become synonymous with pure evil. What many of us often forget however, is that Hitler was not only a stone cold tyrant, he was also a brilliant persuader of the masses. He personally oversaw the murder of millions upon millions of people, including the near extermination of the Jewish race while at the same time maintaining the full support of the German people.

The entire German population could not have been as heartless and as cruel as Hitler was, so it stands to reason that Hitler must have been a masterful propagandist in order to persuade an entire nation that his policies were absolutely necessary and just. Yet, one must remember that Hitler was not born the evil, vicious dictator that he became. His life was governed by both his choices and his life experiences, so it is important to examine these along with his persuasive method to gain a comprehensive understanding of why and how he used his gifts of persuasion in the way that he did.

After becoming the supreme leader, Adolf Hitler began to systematically take away rights while also removing his opposition whenever they arose. In order to be absolutely certain that none of his generals would attempt a coup against him, he gave them all overlapping spheres of power and authority so that they would fight amongst themselves, ensuring that none of them would ever gain enough power to overthrow him.

Hitler used his many years of experience studying human behavior to manipulate people for his own benefit, by unleashing his Nazi propaganda upon all of the German people. It was not until he was Supreme Leader that his persuasive abilities were fully realized. Hitler's persuasive method was built upon the foundation of treating the German people as a group, rather than as individuals. His Nazi Party treated the Germans as if they were one being, mainly because individuals are rational, think for themselves, and are concerned about their own well-being, but groups of people are mostly unorganized making them more susceptible to the laws of social proof.

The Nazis recognized that if the German populace had a group mentality they would be much more receptive to Nazi ideology and propaganda. To reinforce this ideology the Supreme Leader held events that required mass participation such as "parades, mass meetings and semi-religious rituals. Those who did not openly participate or share the emotion of the rest of the crowd were easily identified and dealt with by either the crowd itself or by security personnel. In fact an individual did not even have to be resistant or cause a disturbance to be viewed as subversive. Although Hitler and his Nazi Thugs victimized an entire continent and exterminated millions in their quest for a "Master Race" this concept of genetic selection did not actually originate with Hitler. The idea was conceived in America, to be more exact it was cultivated in California under the name of Eugenics, decades before Adolf Hitler came to power.

The Californian eugenics movement played a very important role in the United States eugenics campaign for ethnic cleansing. Eugenics was a racist pseudoscience which was determined to wipe out all human beings deemed "unworthy," preserving only those who conformed to a Nordic stereotype. In fact, Elements of the philosophy were enshrined as national policy by forcing sterilization and segregation laws as well as marriage restrictions. Many of you may not know this but in 1909 California became the third state to pass such laws. Ultimately practitioners of eugenics coercively sterilized over 10,000 Americans while also legally barring the marriage of thousands of "unworthy" couples. Before the Second World War, nearly half of coercive sterilizations were done in California. Extensive financing by corporate philanthropists is what made the movement so popular, titans of industry such as Dale Carnegie and the Rockefellers all jumped on the Eugenics bandwagon, and they weren't the only ones. These tycoons were all in league with some of the United Sates most trusted researchers and scientists hailing from such prestigious universities as Princeton, Yale and Stanford. In the early 1900's, the Carnegies even established a laboratory on Long Island that kept thousands of files on average

Americans who were possible candidates for sterilization.

The Nazi's quest for a "master race" could not have been possible without the eugenics movement. Race science, racial purity and racial dominance became the driving force behind Adolf Hitler's Nazism. Nazi eugenics would ultimately dictate how non Germans would live and how they would die. Because of this Germany's scientists would become the unseen generals in Hitler's bloody crusade against those he deemed unworthy. Nazi Doctors would create the science, devise the formulas and even hand-select the victims for sterilization, euthanasia and mass extermination. During the Nazi Parties' early years, eugenicists in the United States applauded Hitler's plan as the logical realization of their own years of research and effort. California eugenicists even arranged for Nazi scientific exhibits, such as the famous 1934 showing at the Los Angeles County Museum.

After the war and the fall of the Nazi Party, eugenics was declared a crime against humanity, and was outlawed in the United States. After the laws were changed, California eugenicists renamed their crusade "human genetics" and in 1949 they formed the American Society of Human Genetics. As of today, human genetics' diabolical roots in eugenics are widely unknown by the general populace, but not forgotten. In fact governors of the original five states which publicly practiced eugenics, including California have since issued public apologies to their citizens, past and present, for the abuses spawned by the eugenics movement.

6
Emotional Repatterning

Aside from using eugenics as a platform to attract people to his cause, Hitler did in fact pioneer a wide variety of mass persuasion techniques which now constitutes what many professionals today have come to call "Emotional Repatterning." It's also known as "thought reform," "hypnotic programming", "mental conditioning," and "mind control". These techniques involve the systematic breakdown of a person's sense of self.

In the 1970's Publishing heiress Patty Hearst became a famous victim of these insidious methods when she was kidnapped by the Symbionese Liberation Army, which has come to be known as sort of a "political cult". Hearst was imprisoned in a dark room for several days and was kept hungry and tired. She was also brutalized and made afraid for her life while cult members overwhelmed her with their anti-capitalist ideology. Within two months of her abduction, Patty had changed her name and publicly renounced her family.

Emotional Repatterning is an umbrella term for any myriad of techniques used to get people to behave in ways which normally would contradict their values, beliefs and personal preferences. The concept of "Repatterning" is a very controversial one, most psychologists today believe that cult brainwashing techniques, which are similar to techniques used in prisoner interrogation, do change a person's thought processes.

There is no particular 'personality' that is susceptible to cult mind control techniques. However there are certain characteristics that make people more vulnerable. For example, people who are dependent, unassertive or have a low tolerance for ambiguity, also people who are idealistic or have a strong desire for spiritual meaning are also somewhat susceptible.

Most people will find, on reflection, that there have been times in their lives when they have experienced several or all of these things themselves. This means that everyone is susceptible to being recruited into a cult. If a troubled person happens to encounter a cult member at a time when they are vulnerable and the cult member is offering exactly what they want, like, a relief to their heartache, a new perspective or a way to numb their sorrows, then this gives the cult member the upper hand. Another very important point that makes people incredibly susceptible is an ignorance of how emotional repatterning actually works.

Further Applications of Repatterning

Did you know that large cults even have training manuals which teach the members what kind of people to recruit? For example, a cult may want 'pay-as-you-go' members, people who are earning money and can afford to pay for courses, which always seem to get, more and more expensive. Cult manuals often assist in training new members on how and where to find recruits, how to assess the recruits, and based on the assessment what story to tell to attract possible recruits to a course. Once an individual joins the cause, the cult then uses techniques such as manipulation, blackmail, verbal and physical abuse, forced drug addiction and hypnotic programming to keep their members from leaving or rebelling.

Cults are not the only ones which have used these techniques for destructive purposes. In the early 1960's Dr. Ewen Cameron, a psychiatrist who had served as President of the Canadian Psychiatric Association, secretly conducted experiments that devastated lives and changed the course of psychology forever. Ewen Cameron's experiments initially known as Subproject 68, were partially funded by the CIA and the Canadian government, and are widely known for their use of LSD, barbiturates, and amphetamines on patients.

In the media, they were known as the "mind control" studies and were reported as just one in a series of repatterning projects led by the American and Canadian governments. Decades later, in the 1980s, past victims spoke out about their experiences, and by the 1990's the lawsuits began to pile up. In response, the Canadian government launched "The Allan Memorial Institute Depatterned Persons Assistance Plan," which provided over $100,000 to each of the former patients of Dr. Cameron.

Cameron's experiments were only a fraction of Emotional Repatterning experiments being conducted by The United States and Canada. With the freedom of information act, a myriad of files describing mind control programs were exposed, with names like Project: Bluebird, Operation: Artichoke and Project: MK-ULTRA. These names came to the public's attention in the late 1970's, exposing everyone to the reality and danger of this techniques.

7

American Mind Control

Immediately after World War II, nearly every country on the planet was in a desperate race against time to snatch up and recruit former Nazi scientists, doctors, builders and military strategists. In the United States the CIA with permission from President Truman, launched Operation: Paperclip, a top secret government program designed to expedite the citizenship of hundreds of Nazi personnel, giving them new identities and placing them in top tier positions in Government programs including NASA's rocket program.

To cover their tracks the Central Intelligence Agency destroyed all files which included Nazi references, names, birthdays and former occupations. By the mid 1950's, more than 700 German scientists had been granted citizenship in the U.S. and were given prominent positions in the scientific community. Many former Nazis even became employed CIA agents, engaging in clandestine work with the likes of the NSA and Henry Kissinger.

This is but one of many results of Operation: Paperclip. As The U.S. began research into emotional repatterning, mind control, thought reform and hypnotic programming a program under Operation: Paperclip called Project: MK Ultra was created. The researchers who participated in the project, which included Dr. Ewen Cameron in Canada, used some of the same techniques as the Nazi gestapo.

These methods included electro shock, sleep deprivation, memory implantation, memory erasure, sensory modification and psychotropic drug experiments. At the very beginning of the project in the early 1950's government operatives began studying hypnosis and concluded that they could not make people do things against their will. Subjects in the experiments who were put into a hypnotic trance would refuse to hurt themselves or inflict pain onto others. However, the experimenters found that they could circumvent resistance by convincing people that the person they were told to harm was actually a deadly enemy who threatened the lives of their families. By changing their perception of reality, the experimenters created what they called a "dual-reality". MK Ultra scientists soon came to the conclusion that if they could create the right reality for the subject, than they could manipulate people into doing almost anything.

Soon the United States Government granted the CIA permission to develop projects designed to control perception on various levels. Experiments ranged from dosing individuals with LSD to kidnapping unsuspecting citizens right off the streets forcibly injecting them with drugs, one such subproject of MK Ultra called Project Midnight Climax included such methods and was conducted in various CIA rented hotel rooms in New York and San Francisco.

The perception-altering properties of LSD and other psychoactive drugs fit well with the CIA's agenda. The government agency focused on a three pronged approach for psychoactive drug experiments, which started with "truth serums" that could be used during interrogation, then drugs that could induce amnesia, and lastly emotional repatterning techniques that could create what is often described as a "Manchurian Candidate", named after the famous Frank Sinatra picture of the 1960's which centered on mind controlled soldiers.

In pursuit of these goals MK Ultra researchers tested dozens upon dozens of psychoactive, chemicals ,including, dimethyltryptamine, ecstasy, heroin, marijuana, and phencyclidine. They particularly focused on Lysergic Acid Diethylamide or LSD for short, funneling millions of dollars through covert channels into drug studies at clinics and hospitals. In fact, the research into LSD's pharmacology conducted in the late 1950s was mostly funded by the U.S. military and the Central Intelligence Agency. The MK Ultra Program was discontinued in 1972 after more than 20 years of illegal testing, and many of its cousins including Operation Midnight Climax and Project: Bluebird a Navy based experiment were also discontinued.

In the late 1970's with the freedom of information act many of these files were exposed creating a public outcry, causing the government to launch a full investigation into the projects notorious activities. CIA director Sidney Gottlieb was given full immunity from prosecution during the trial in exchange for providing testimony. Until this day no employee of the CIA has ever been terminated for dosing subjects with LSD without their knowledge, and despite the public reaction and media frenzy surrounding the experiments no criminal charges have ever been filed related to Operation Midnight Climax, Project: Bluebird or Project: MK Ultra.

8

Following Authority

In the mid-1960s' brilliant psychologist Stanley Milgram began researching the effects of authority on obedience. The main question which got the ball rolling in Milgram's mind was "could what happened in Hitler's Germany happen here in the United States"? After his experiment's Milgram concluded that people obey either out of fear or out of a desire to appear cooperative, even when acting against their own better judgment. Stanley Milgram's eye opening yet controversial experiment illustrates people's reluctance to confront those who abuse power. Milgram recruited participants for his experiments from various walks in life. Subjects were told the experiment would study the effects of punishment on learning ability, and as an extra incentive they were offered cash for participating in the experiment. Although subjects thought they had an equal chance of playing the role of a student or of a teacher, the process was rigged so everyone ended up playing the teacher, while the learner was actually a paid actor working as a cohort of the experimenter. Upon the start, the "teachers" were asked to administer increasingly severe electric shocks to the "learner" when questions were answered incorrectly. Yet, in reality, the only electric shocks delivered in the experiment were single 45-volt shock samples given to each teacher. This was done to give the teachers a feeling for the shocks that they would supposeably be discharging during the course of the experiment.

    To further convince outsiders of the legitimacy of the experiment shock levels were labeled from 15 to 450 volts. Beginning from the lower end, jolt levels were labeled: "slight shock," "moderate shock," "strong shock," "very strong shock," "intense shock," and "extreme intensity shock." Then to increase intensity in the teacher's reality, the next two levels were labeled "Danger: Severe Shock," and, past that, a simple but ghastly

"XXX" appeared. In response to the supposed shocks, the "learner" (actor) would start to grunt at 75 volts; complain at 120 volts; ask to be let go at 150 volts and let out painful shouts at 285 volts. Eventually, in desperation, the learner was to yell loudly and complain of possible heart problems and chest pains. At one point the "learner" would refuse to answer any more questions. Then, at 300 volts the "learner" would secretly be instructed to remain silent for the rest of the experiment that is of course if any of the teacher participants got so far without rebelling.

To further elevate stress levels teachers were instructed to treat any silence as an incorrect answer and apply the next shock level to the "learner". If at any point the teacher hesitated to inflict the jolts, the experimenter would pressure them to proceed without fail. Such demands from the researchers would take the form of increasingly severe statements, such as "The experiment requires that you continue with your work." Now, what do you think was the average voltage given by teachers before they refused to administer future jolts? What percentage of teachers, if any, do you think went up to the maximum voltage of 450? Well, I'll tell you, some teachers refused to continue with the jolts very early on, despite urging from the researchers. This is the type of response Milgram expected as the norm, but Milgram was shocked to find those who questioned authority were actually in the minority.

Exactly 65% of the teachers were willing to progress to the maximum voltage level of XXX. Nearly all subjects during the course of the experiment demonstrated a wide range of negative emotions about continuing. Several of the "teachers" even attempted to help the "learner", by telling them to answer questions carefully, and surprisingly enough, others even broke out in nervous laughter.

A few of the subjects even appeared stoic, hopeless, somber, or arrogant.. Nevertheless, subjects continued to participate, discharging the full array of jolts to the learners. One man in particular, who wanted to abandon the experiment was told point blank "the experiment must continue, no matter what". Instead of challenging the decision of the experimenter, the man proceeded, repeating to himself loudly, "It's got to continue, it's got to continue." Milgram's experiment also included a number of variations. In one, the "learner" or paid actor was not only visible but teachers were asked to force the learner's hand to the shock plate so that they could deliver the punishment. The result was that a lot less obedience was extracted from participants in that variation. Seeing the "learner" during the experiment ended up triggering a strong since of empathy causing the subjects to stop.

In yet another variation of the experiment, Subjects were instructed to apply whatever voltage they desired to incorrect answers. Teachers averaged 80 volts, and only 2.5 percent of participants used the full 450 volts available. This showed that most participants were good, average people, not evil sadists. After the experiment participants were debriefed and showed much relief at finding out they had not actually harmed anyone. One such man in particular cried from emotion when he saw the "learner" alive, and explained that he thought he had murdered him.

Milgram's Shocking Results

So, what was the difference between those who obeyed and those who rebelled? Milgram divided the subjects into three categories. First there was the group he called "Obeyed and Justified". Some obedient subjects gave up all responsibility for their actions, blaming the researcher. Others had actually transferred the blame to the learner, often saying: "He was so dumb and stubborn that he deserved to be shocked."

The second category Milgram labeled as "Obeyed and blamed themselves". In this group the subjects felt badly about what they had done and were quite harsh on themselves. Members of this group would, perhaps, be more likely to challenge authority if confronted with a similar situation in the future.

Lastly there was the group which was simply called "Rebellious". Rebellious subjects questioned the authority of the experimenter and argued there was a greater ethical calling for the protection of the learner over the needs of the experimenter. Some of these individuals felt they were accountable to a higher authority.

This groundbreaking experiment shows how blindly people follow perceived authority figures. In fact, this is just one of the many techniques "con-artists" use when trying to convince a target, they project confident authority without fail. By understanding this I hope that in the future you will become more aware of this outrageous misperception and simply ask yourself "Do I actually agree with this person's philosophy or am I just blindly following authority".

9

The Social Brain

I don't know if you aware of this but there is an invisible epidemic that is affecting millions of Americans, it is called loneliness. Don't get me wrong everyone gets lonely at times, but consistent loneliness poses a serious health risk, in fact, it's now been proven that loneliness and social isolation are as much a threat to your daily health as obesity, alcohol and drug abuse. In my opinion I believe that men and women need to attend to loneliness in the same way they would their diet, exercise, or how much sleep they get every night.

The effects of social isolation or even rejection are as real as thirst, hunger, or pain. We live in a social world and to be on the edge of that social perimeter is to be in a very dangerous position. When your brain is on high alert, your body responds in kind. Morning levels of the stress hormone cortisol go up when you are mentally preparing for another stressful day. This chemical entrainment sets a baseline for what your day will be like, as the day goes on and we reach bedtime, the cortisol bath swirling around inside our bodies not only disrupts our sleep cycles, it can also create chronic insomnia. Loneliness can also alter gene expressions, deciding for us what genes are turned on and off.

Animal studies in loneliness have shown that social isolation also alters levels of dopamine, which as I mentioned in previous chapters is a neurotransmitter that determines impulsive behavior. This combination of chemical reactions can impair cognitive performance, compromise the immune system, and increase the risk for vascular, inflammatory, and heart disease. Loneliness also increases the risk of early death by 45% and also ups the chance of developing dementia in later life by 64%. Individuals who have stronger social ties to family, friends and community are 50% less at risk of developing chronic illnesses.

There's nothing wrong with feeling lonely, at times, it is perfectly common for people to experience loneliness when their social networks are shifting, like starting a new job or moving to a new town, but there is a big difference between temporary "states" and chronic "states" of loneliness.

A lack social skills or an inability to relate to others more often than not trigger feelings of isolation, which is why I always encourage my clients to be aware how exactly to create instant rapport with another individual. Rapport is a feeling of trust and confidence that you get when you speak with someone and really connect with them, and soon you begin feeling like you have known them for a long time, even if you have only just met them. Rapport is simply that strange and subtle feeling that you really like somebody.

When you're in rapport with someone, your bodies and voices will match. If you can learn to create rapport with people more easily, you'll make more friends, do better in business and best of all, learn to understand people better. One way to create rapport is by matching the other person's body language. By mirroring the way they carry themselves, you are communicating to their subconscious that "I am just like you!" People definitely like people who are like themselves, so this is a great way to get along with someone new and stop feelings of loneliness before they have a chance to start.

Please note, matching body language is not mimicry. You don't just copy every little movement the other person makes. You have to be subtle, otherwise people are going to think that you are insensitive, deranged or just rude. To create rapport, see the other person's body language as a dance, a dance where they take the lead. Dance with them by matching their body language, but do so delicately. An easy way to do this is by matching posture.

If you're sitting with someone and they are crossing their legs, it's fine to cross yours in the same way. If they lean forwards when they speak, you can lean forwards too. If they start to lean back, feel free to do so accordingly. As a guide, I normally wait 20 seconds or so before matching somebody's body language, as your movement is much less likely to be consciously picked up on. It feels more natural and less forced that way too.

It goes without saying that facial gestures can be matched inoffensively. For example, if somebody smiles at you, it's perfectly fine to smile back immediately. If they play with their hair, or twiddle a pen, you can do so too, just try not to make too big a deal of it. All of these little gestures will be picked up by the other person's subconscious, and will affirm the belief that you are just like them, so they are worth playing with.

Creating rapport with body language gets a little trickier when you attempt to match smaller movements that the other person makes. When you try this, you have to be a little more sensitive. For example, if the other person moves their arm, you can match this by gently moving your hand on the corresponding side in the same direction. If they move their body, match by moving or nodding your head to follow the direction they take. It's almost as if you make a little "tribute" move for every larger move that they make. You can even attempt to match breathing with the other person, i.e. breathe at the same speed and at the same depth that they do.

Pacing

Rapport is established and maintained by pacing. By definition, this is the process of moving as the other person moves. Pacing or matching accepts the other person's behavior and meets them in their model of the world. It is about reducing the differences between yourself and others at an unconscious level. You can pace or match many different aspects of behavior. Of course, if the other person is aware you are matching their behavior it becomes mimicry. Obvious attempts to "copy" people will break rapport. Successful pacing is at an unconscious tool.

Voice
Matching the pace, volume, pitch, tone and type of words is a little tricky to learn but worth it. Try watching a TV program in a foreign language in order to notice these auditory processing distinctions. You don't have to try to match all these aspects. Choose one. If a person is talking slowly, slow down. If they speak softly, drop your volume.

Beliefs and Values
Authentically trying to understand another person's beliefs and values without judgment can create very deep rapport. Once again, you do not have to agree with them or change any of your own values; the goal is to understand.

Now, I'll discuss getting in rapport with difficult people. Hostile personalities are those who obviously oppose your ideas and hold their own opposing views. As a result of your differences with the other person you may find that hostile people will question your credibility, evidence and open-mindedness. They will believe that they are right, and that you are wrong. In addition, because we tend to dislike people who hold viewpoints that oppose or challenge our own, you may even experience verbal or physical abuse. Persuading an openly hostile opponent must therefore be done extremely carefully and with caution. Use the wrong tactic or try to persuade too quickly, and you will only succeed in entrenching them in their original belief. Remember they believe that you are wrong and they are right, so you need to persuade them in a simple, gentle, non-threatening and convincing way.

To begin persuading an explosive personality, you first need to warm them up to the point where they will listen to you and consider your points. If you can't get them to listen, then you won't be able to persuade them. A good tactic for establishing rapport is to begin with a neutral joke or story, in other words, a pattern interrupt. This will confuse them and it will lower their defenses. Then start talking about the areas you already agree on, or things which you have in common, remember people like those who are like themselves. The more similar they think you are to them the more they will like you, the more they will listen to you and the more likely it will be that you can persuade them later on. When you begin to use any persuasion technique, don't start with a direct attack such as by telling the person they are wrong or why you think they are wrong. Also don't begin by stating that you are going to change their mind about an issue. If you do any of these all you will do is blow your chances and break rapport. The best way to approach a hostile person is to try to establish some degree of credibility. You can do this by stating the negatives about your own point of view, whilst at the same time mentioning the positives about their particular point of view. This is a great approach because you are not attacking, but instead are telling them what they already know and agree with it.

Now that you have approached the subject you can begin to challenge their point of view, and perhaps, persuade them to your way of thinking. When stating opposing points of view, always ensure that your statements are supported by a credible source. This could include experts, people who you both know or sources such as the news or scientific papers. Make sure you don't over exaggerate. When presenting your evidence, try to stress that you are looking for a win-win solution. Psychologically a win-win solution is less threatening, as some people do not like to admit that their original belief was wrong for fear of looking foolish. Although in some cases you may not always be able to offer a win-win solution. In which case, you need to present very strong supporting evidence which makes your proposal the only sensible course of action to follow and stress the benefits that will come from following it.

Yet, some people just don't like to admit they are wrong, especially if they have held a particular belief for a long period of time. They have become entrenched in a particular viewpoint, and do not want to change it no matter what you say.

When presented with convincing solid evidence these types of people will just choose to ignore the information, or make fun of it. This is called cognitive dissonance and describes how people become extremely reluctant to change their views because it would mean changing their entire belief systems. So if you are trying to persuade a very hostile or head strong person, be prepared to hang in there for a long run as you may need several attempts before you are finally able to persuade them. But stick to it, because at the end of the day everyone can be persuaded, no matter what, some just take longer than others.

The truth is, some people are naturally suspicious of other people, especially if they do not know them. Because of this suspicion, you may find that people will try to test you during your conversations with them. For example they will try to reveal bias in your information or discover what you personally stand to gain.

If a person thinks that your message is heavily biased, then they will carefully analyze what you are saying and will probably dismiss it. This is because information which is perceived as being biased is also usually perceived as being a threat, because in most cases, biased information will result in one person gaining at another person's expense. Because acting in your own self-interest only causes a perceived lack of trust, one way that persuaders can appear to be more trustworthy is by doing the opposite and acting against their own self-interest. If we are convinced that someone has nothing to gain from their actions, or perhaps even something to lose, then we are much more likely to see that person as trustworthy. One of the absolute best ways to increase trustworthiness and decrease bias, is to convince the other person that you are not trying to persuade them.

What it comes down to folks, is that loneliness is a choice. Solitude can be good at times, it can be healthy and healing, but isolation is destructive. When you isolate yourself, you lose touch with reality. Cutting yourself off from relationships that give life can expose you to life threatening conditions such as depression and anxiety which ultimately shortens your lifespan.

10
Hypnotherapy and NLP

As a Hypnotherapist I've heard everything from hypnosis is not real to it's a tool for evil. Through all my years in this field I can honestly say that hypnosis is real, and is a very powerful tool for change. Like any powerful tool in the wrong hands it can repair of destroy, it all depends on the intention and moral judgments of the user. You see, everyone goes into hypnosis every single day, it's called a "trance state". Between the ages of 0 and 6, a child is in a period of super learning, in other words they spend the first years of their lives in a state of hypnosis. This is how a baby learns how to smile, talk, walk and reason. They model the people around them constantly taking in suggestion after suggestion until they develop their own personalities which is usually around 7 or 8 years of age.

In order to fully understand what hypnosis is, one must consider the inner workings of the mind. Our mind functions in four different levels of activity. The first level is called beta. This is the stage of complete consciousness. We function in this level for approximately sixteen hours a day. When you go to sleep, your brain automatically cycles down from the beta range into the alpha.

Alpha corresponds to the subconscious mind and is what is dealt with in hypnosis. Other examples of activity in this stage are meditation, daydreaming, biofeedback and natural sleep. When you're inebriated either by drugs or lack of sleep your mind naturally goes into alpha, which is why when a patient is in surgery it is natural practice for doctors to request long bouts of silence because it is understood that this is when the mind is most vulnerable to verbal suggestion.

After the alpha state we go into theta. All of our emotional experiences seem to be recorded in theta. Theta is that special range that opens the door of consciousness beyond hypnosis into the world of psychic phenomena, like astral projection and remote viewing. The last stage is called delta. This corresponds to deep sleep. Here is where the subconscious mind is obtaining the greatest amount of rest. Suggestions will not be heard at this level. This level lasts approximately thirty to forty minutes each night.

There are many serious misperceptions about hypnosis. Many of these have been promoted by movies or TV shows which depict people being transformed into zombie like creatures by some mystic who says, "Look into my eyes!". While this may makes for some exciting entertainment, it is 100 percent fictional and has no resemblance to the truth. Here's another one, have you ever heard someone say that a hypnotist possesses mystical abilities. Hypnotists are ordinary people who have mastered the skill of using the power of suggestion to bring someone into the alpha level, that's all there is to it. A person cannot be hypnotized and made to do things against his or her will either.

All hypnosis is self-hypnosis. During hypnosis, the subject can choose to accept or reject any suggestion given. If a suggestion is given that upsets the subject, this will create a "break of state" and will snap someone out of hypnosis immediately using their own free will. Under hypnosis a person is very aware of where he or she is and what is happening. The subject hears everything and is in a dreamlike state of deep relaxation. Often the subject has either a numbness throughout the body or no acute awareness of having a body.

Hypnotherapy can be a highly effective form of treatment for many mental, psychosomatic, and physical disorders. For example, through the use of regressive techniques, a patient may mentally voyage back to a point in their youth that was particularly troublesome, allowing the healing of old emotional wounds. Another patient can be led to understand that emotional pain has been converted to physical pain, and that the pain can be eliminated once the source has been addressed. A person suffering from chronic pain can be taught to control the pain without the use of medications, it can also be useful when a patient is allergic to a particular type of anesthesia. In hypnotherapy there are a number of methods for correcting dysfunctional behaviors such as self-destructive habits, anxiety disorders, and it even helps someone in managing side effects of various medical treatments and procedures.

Through my practice I have personally used therapeutic hypnosis to curb the urge to eat for overeaters, to eliminate the disruptive actions of obsessive compulsive disorders, cure insomnia and minimize stress. Excessive stress can be generated from any number of sources and can be the springboard for anxiety. Some of the more prominent sources of anxiety and stress for which people seek hypnotherapy are: public speaking, test taking, and job stress. Hypnotherapy also works well for other anxiety disorders such as phobias and has proven to be an effective treatment for mild to moderate depression.

Hypnotherapy has also been used in conjunction with traditional cognitive behavioral therapy, to help individuals who had severe aversion to needles. In my opinion treatments like this are necessary especially for those who absolutely require periodic medical injections, like diabetics. In terminally ill cancer patients, it has also been concluded that hypnotherapy is much more effective at enhancing quality of life and relieving depressive symptoms, when compared to others who received traditional care. One of the best possible applications for hypnosis that I have found is in guided visual therapy. This is where you, the hypnotist, guides someone through a visual depiction or scenario in which they can imagine themselves free of the problem or in the case of sports hypnosis, picture themselves succeeding at a high level. This approach is particularly favored in the sporting world as it has been proven to greatly increase concentration, self-confidence, determination and performance.

In all my years as a hypnotherapist the most common use of therapeutic hypnosis is smoking cessation. Cigarette smoking can be a behavioral problem or it can be a true addiction. In most cases, it is a little of both. The physiological craving is gone after about seven days of not smoking, but the psychological craving, which can be just as strong, persists much longer.

If you feel you are addicted and want to use a nicotine patch or one of the new drugs prescribed or recommended by a doctor, I recommend you do self-hypnosis along with it. After all, you have to contend with the long-term craving that usually persists after you quit. Hypnosis is one of the most effective ways to quit smoking. Even the Surgeon General's report on smoking noted that hypnosis could be effective. There are many hypnotists today, including myself who conduct group therapy sessions for ex-smokers which have produced long lasting positive effects.

Hypnotherapy can also be an invaluable tool when you want to discover how to build self-confidence. This is because going into hypnosis allows you to step out of your everyday way of thinking and feeling about yourself and your life. When you are deeply relaxed, and listening to empowering suggestions crafted by skilled and experienced hypnotherapists, you naturally become more flexible and creative.

The second greatest tool that I have used to induce rapid and incredible change in my clients is what is called Neuro Linguistic Programming or NLP for short. For those you are unfamiliar with it, Neuro Linguistic Programming is a methodology based on the presupposition that all behavior has a structure that can be modeled, learned, taught and changed.

Neuro stands for the nervous system and our mind in which our external experiences are received and processed through the five senses. Linguistic is for the verbal and nonverbal communication systems through which our neural experiences are coded, ordered and given meaning. Programming is the ability to discover and utilize the programs that we run in our neurological systems to achieve desired out comes. It is our ability to organize our verbal and nonverbal communication patterns.

I have personally studied, applied and trained people in NLP for several years now and am completely convinced it is one of the most effective ways to initiate quick and lasting change in people. It has been used all over the world to transform fear, stress, hate, depression and anxiety into confidence, relaxation, love and euphoria. Through all my time as a Hypnotherapist, Life Coach and Motivational Speaker I've met countless individuals who tell me that things don't seem to look any better when they glance into their future. If you begin to change the way in which you visualize your own destiny, this drastically changes the emotions you produce. Many people think that if other people changed, then they would be happy, but in fact that's not true at all, you either know how to be happy or you don't.

If you feel bad it is because you are picturing bad events and you also might be speaking to yourself negatively. For sadness to happen in your body, you have to focus on specific images, hold your body in a slumped position and talk to yourself in a certain way. All the negative emotions I have already mentioned are nothing but reinforced habits that have become automatic. If you change the way you talk to yourself, change the kind of pictures you make in your mind and In fact the way in which you have feelings, then you can build new habits

In Conclusion

Nearly a decade ago I launched into a mission of self-discovery that profoundly changed my life forever. Some of my greatest difficulties early on in life stemmed from the fact that I truly didn't understand human behavior. How can a person be one way one minute and completely different the next. What made it worse was that growing up I never had access to the wide range of free information that is now available to today's youth.

In fact, when I was a teenager the internet didn't even exist, dial up connections were barely functional and giant clunky flip cell phones were all the rage. My journey to find the answers I was seeking took this lonely California boy to new and exotic places like, Australia, Singapore, Malaysia, Hong Kong and Alaska just to name a few. The one answer that kept popping up everywhere was that we are a lot more alike than we care to admit.

After years of research I found that truly understanding human behavior is absolutely essential for anyone looking to cultivate positive relationships with others and avoid unnecessary conflict.

I have also come to strongly believe that the study of human behavior needs to be part of the regular educational curriculum in our public schools today. So much of the pain and heartache that our young people go through is due in large part to a lack of proper guidance and support. Teaching our younger generation about the complexities of behavior helps give them a better understanding of the fact that we are always in control of how we react to things.

The Learning Process

You see, there are four stages of learning that govern our lives. First there is Unconscious incompetence, which is not knowing that you don't know. Then there's conscious incompetence, this is where you know that you don't know. After reading this book and consistently applying the information to better your life you will graduate to the level of a conscious competent. In this stage you know want to do, you put it into action and you start to achieve your goals. Mental strength and momentum also start to accumulate as you navigate through obstacles and hardships. The next level is where true professionals live, this is where dreams are manifested into reality. This stage is described as unconscious competence. When you have saturated your brain with consistent information to the point where a response becomes automatic, then you have arrived at unconscious competence.

The conscious mind is logical. It has the ability to think, reason, criticize, analyze, judge, choose, select, discriminate, plan, invent and compose, use hindsight and foresight. It uses both deductive and inductive reasoning. The conscious mind, for the most part, filters the impact of input to the subconscious mind. Everything gets into the subconscious mind, but the conscious mind can influence the effect. Our conscious minds do not begin to develop until the age of three and it is not fully developed until about the age of 20. Thus, most people have a lot of garbage in their subconscious minds, which is counterproductive to their health, peace of mind, and productivity.

The subconscious mind, on the other hand, is not logical, it is the feeling mind. It is the source of love, hatred, anguish, fear, jealousy, sadness, anger, joy and desire. When you say, "I feel..." the source of the feeling is the subconscious mind. Think of an extreme example, such as rage. A person expressing deep rage exhibits strong emotion, superior strength, is highly illogical, and has poor recollection of his or her behavior afterward. When your conscious mind and your subconscious mind are in conflict, your subconscious mind wins, but only if you do not know how to control it.

The absolute best way for managing change in your behavior relates to the belief of 'positive intention'. This principle is especially valuable when dealing with resistances and objections. The principle essentially states that, "at some level, all behavior is intended or has been developed for some positive purpose".

According to this principle, resistances or objections would actually emerge from some underlying positive intention or purpose. For example, the positive purpose behind the objection, "It is not desirable to be successful," may be to actually "guard" the speaker from oversaturation or failure. The positive intention behind a resistance such as, "people never change," might be to prevent false hope or to avoid unrewarded effort.

The principle of positive intention states that, in order to successfully change a resistance or limiting belief, these underlying concerns, or positive purposes, must be acknowledged and addressed in some way. The positive intention behind a resistance or limiting belief may be addressed directly or by widening the person's map of the situation such that they are able to see choices for satisfying their positive intent other than resistance or interference. The principle of positive intention is derived from the deeper assumption that people make the best choices available to them given the possibilities and capabilities that they perceive to be accessible within their model of the world. Through personal experience I have found that Hypnosis and Neuro Linguistic Programing are the absolute best ways to help people expand their map of a situation in order to perceive other choices and options.

Yet, another powerful way to control the unconscious process, as I mentioned before is to practice your desired behavior daily until it becomes an automatic response. I can't stress enough the importance of repetition, this may be a time consuming task but it's completely worth it.

It is my hope that this book will serve as a stepping stone for your own journey of self-discovery. Having a strong grasp of human dynamics and self-awareness early on can help one cope with one's emotions positively. We should all study human behavior to maintain positive social relations with others and to aide in creating a harmoniously joyful society.

Glossary

Anchoring: The process of associating an internal response with some external trigger so that the response may be quickly recreated.

Auditory: Relating to hearing or the sense of hearing.

Behavior: The specific physical actions and reactions through which we interact with the people and environment around us.

Behavioral Flexibility: The ability to vary one's own behavior in order to elicit or secure a response from another person.

Beliefs: Closely held generalizations about cause, meaning and boundaries in the world around us. Beliefs function at a different level than concrete reality and serve to guide and interpret our perceptions of reality, often by connecting them to our criteria or value systems.

Calibration: The process of learning to read another person's unconscious, non-verbal responses in an ongoing interaction by pairing observable behavioral cues with a specific internal response.

Capability: Mastery over an entire class of behavior. Knowing how to do something. Capabilities come from the development of a mental map that allows us to select and organize groups of individual behaviors.

Congruence: When all of a person's internal beliefs, strategies and behaviors are fully in agreement and oriented toward securing a desired outcome.

Context: The framework surrounding a particular event. This framework will often determine how a particular experience or event is interpreted.

Emotional Repatterning: Any myriad of techniques used to get people to behave in ways which normally would contradict their values, beliefs and personal preferences.

Environment: The external context in which our behavior takes place. Our environment is that which we perceive as being "outside" of us. It is not part of our behavior but it is rather something we must react to.

Installation: The process of facilitating the acquisition of a new strategy or behavior. A new strategy may be installed through some combination of anchoring, accessing cues, metaphor and future pacing.

Kinesthetic: Relating to body sensations. In NLP the term kinesthetic is used to encompass all kinds of feelings including tactile and emotional.

Metaphor: The process of thinking about one situation or phenomenon as something else.

Mind Control: Encompasses a series of methods in which human beings can be indoctrinated in ways that cause an inability to think independently while also causing a massive disruption of core values and beliefs

MK Ultra: The code name given to an illegal CIA run program which experimented on unsuspecting citizens during the 1950' through the early 1970's.

The program's main intention was to develop drugs and procedures to be used in interrogations and torture in order to weaken the individual and force confessions through coercive techniques.

Neuro Linguistic Programming: The study of how words and images effect a person's nervous system and emotions. NLP studies the patterns created by the interaction among the brain, language and the body that produce both effective and ineffective behavior.

Neuro-Linkages: The links between thoughts and emotions in our minds, which create and shape our behaviors and performance results.

Outcomes: Goals or desired states that a person or organization aspires to achieve.

Pacing: A method used by communicators to quickly establish rapport by matching certain aspects of their behavior to those of the person with whom they are communicating.

Rapport: The establishment of trust, harmony, and cooperation in a relationship.

State: The total ongoing mental and physical conditions which a person is acting out.

Strategy: A set of explicit mental and behavioral steps used to achieve a specific outcome. In NLP, the most important aspect of a strategy is representational systems used to carry out the specific steps.

Utilization: A technique in which a specific strategy sequence or pattern of behavior is paced or matched in order to influence another's response.

Visual: Relating to sight or the sense of sight.

Well-Formedness Conditions: The set of conditions something must satisfy in order to produce an effective and ecological outcome. In NLP a particular goal is well-formed if it can be: 1) stated in positive terms, 2) defined and evaluated according to sensory based evidence, 3) initiated and maintained by the person who desires the goal, 4) made to preserve the positive byproducts of the present state, and 5) appropriately contextualized to fit the external ecology.

Sources

Bosmajian, Haig A. "Nazi Persuasion and the Crowd Mentality." *Western Speech* 29.2 (1965): 68-78. *Communication & Mass Media Complete*. EBSCO. Web. 25 Jan. 2011.

Braslow, Joel T. 1996. "In the Name of Therapeutics: The Practice of Sterilization in a California State Hospital." *Journal of the History of Medicine & Allied Sciences* 51, 1: 29–51.

Brave, Ralph, and Kathryn Sylva. 2007. "Exhibiting Eugenics: Response and Resistance to a Hidden History." *The Public Historian* 29, 3: 33–51.

Craig, Albert, William Graham, Donald Kagan, Steven Ozment, and Frank Turner. *The Heritage of World Civilizations*. 8th ed. Vol 2. Upper Saddle River, NJ: Pearson Education, 2009. Print. 2 vols.

Currell, Susan, and Christina Cogdell. 2006. *Popular Eugenics*. Athens: Ohio University Press.

Hitler, Adolf." *Encyclopedia Britannica. Encyclopedia Britannica Online*. Encyclopedia Britannica, 2011. Web. 24 Jan. 2011.

"Mein Kampf." *Encyclopedia Britannica. Encyclopedia Britannica Online*. Encyclopedia Britannica, 2011. Web. 27 Jan. 2011.

Milgram, Stanley 1974: obedience to authority. New York: Harper & Row.

About The Author

Rick Camacho is a charismatic Award Winning Public Speaker, Trainer of Neuro Linguistic Programming, Hypnotist, Life Coach and Best Selling Author. A United States Veteran, Rick served honourably in two branches of the Armed Forces, where he honed his cutting edge communication skills and tactics in hostile environments.

Since then, Rick Camacho has gone on to launch the Strategic Empowerment Consultants LLC. As CEO and Co-Founder Rick has developed a number of courses and certifications in subjects ranging from NLP to the Law of Attraction for the sole purpose of assisting people to move beyond their self-imposed limitations so that they may manifest their dreams into reality.

About The Strategic Empowerment Consultants LLC

The Strategic Empowerment Consultants LLC is a training and consulting company based out of Los Angeles, California which specializes in offering certifications and One on One Empowerment sessions in Neuro Linguistic Programing, Hypnosis and life coaching. The Company was Founded by Rick Camacho a Hypnotherapist and Motivational Speaker and Grace Camacho a Business Expert and Communications Consultant with the intent of helping people create an inner alignment of ideas, goals and beliefs, in turn, empowering them to elevate the way they think, speak and ultimately live their lives.

Other Books by Rick Camacho
Now Available on Amazon.com

Neuro Persuasion

Neuro Healing

Master Your Life With NLP: The Easy To Understand Guide to Neuro Linguistic Programming

If you wish to learn more about the author or the Strategic Empowerment Consultants LLC,

Please visit us at
www.strategicempowermentconsultants.com

Made in the USA
Monee, IL
10 March 2021